W9-CEK-165

FREAKY TRUE SCIENCE

FREAKY STORIES WHILE YOU SLEEP

BY CAITIE McANENEY

Gareth Stevens
PUBLISHING

Library of Congress Cataloging-in-Publication Data

Names: McAneney, Caitie, author.
Title: Freaky stories while you sleep / Caitie McAneney.
Other titles: Freaky true science.
Description: New York : Gareth Stevens Publishing, [2017] | Series: Freaky true science | Includes bibliographical references and index.
Identifiers: LCCN 2016000746 | ISBN 9781482448511 (pbk.) | ISBN 9781482448535 (library bound) | ISBN 9781482448528 (6 pack)
Subjects: LCSH: Sleep–Juvenile literature. | Sleep disorders–Juvenile literature.
Classification: LCC RC547 .M425 2017 | DDC 613.7/94–dc23
LC record available at http://lccn.loc.gov/2016000746

First Edition

Published in 2017 by
Gareth Stevens Publishing
111 East 14th Street, Suite 349
New York, NY 10003

Copyright © 2017 Gareth Stevens Publishing

Designer: Sarah Liddell
Editor: Ryan Nagelhout

Photo credits: Cover, p. 1 (bed) lynea/Shutterstock.com; cover, p. 1 (woman) Marcos Mesa Sam Worldley/Shutterstock.com; cover, p. 1 (brain used throughout book) Hein Nouwens/Shutterstock.com; cover, background throughout book Fedorov Oleksiy/Shutterstock.com; pp. 5, 7, 9, 11, 13, 15, 17, 19, 21, 23, 25, 27, 29 (hand used throughout) Helena Ohman/Shutterstock.com; pp. 5, 7, 9, 11, 13, 15, 17, 19, 21, 23, 25, 27, 29 (texture throughout) Alex Gontar/Shutterstock.com; p. 5 Chad Zuber/Shutterstock.com; p. 7 tab62/Shutterstock.com; p. 9 decade3d - anatomy online/Shutterstock.com; p. 11 Mike Focus/Shutterstock.com; p. 13 The Washington Post/Contributor/The Washington Post/Getty Images; p. 15 Sergey Mironov/Shutterstock.com; p. 17 StockLite/Shutterstock.com; p. 19 BFG Images/Getty Images; p. 21 frenky362/Shutterstock.com; p. 23 Ralph Crane/Contributor/The LIFE Picture Collection/Getty Images; p. 25 Antonio Guillem/Shutterstock.com; p. 27 Howard Sandler/Shutterstock.com; p. 29 John Greim/Contributor/LightRocket/Getty Images.

Printed in the United States of America

CPSIA compliance information: Batch #CS16GS: For further information contact Gareth Stevens, New York, New York at 1-800-542-2595.

CONTENTS

Words in the glossary appear in **bold** type
the first time they are used in the text.

WHEN SLEEP GETS FREAKY

Most people spend about one-third of their life asleep. If you're 9 years old, you've already spent about 3 years of your life in bed! For most people, sleep is a way to rest and recharge for the next day. But for others, sleeping can be difficult and even a little freaky.

The brain is an amazing thing. It has several different states, from awake to somewhat asleep to fast asleep and dreaming. As you fall deeper into sleep, your body relaxes and you become unable to move. This is normal, but sometimes transitions, or changes, between waking and sleeping don't go smoothly. This book explores some of the weirdest things people experience from the comfort of their bed and what happens when they leave their bed!

FREAKY FACTS!

Some people suffer from sleep terrors, or night terrors, where they sit up in bed and scream. Even though the person is shouting with their eyes open, they're still stuck in sleep!

NIGHTMARES

One freaky sleep **phenomenon** we've all experienced is nightmares. We spend more than two hours dreaming each night—some of our dreams are bound to be upsetting. When you sleep, your brain gives off chance signals that cause a series of pictures and sounds. Some scientists think dreams are the brain's way of making a story out of these random signals. Nightmares can be scary and make you worry. Others make people feel embarrassed, disgusted, or afraid.

INSOMNIA

Have you ever lain awake in bed long after everyone else has gone to sleep? Have you counted the minutes on the clock, feeling restless? This happens to most people at some point in their lives. You may have trouble sleeping if you're worried about a class or if you're not feeling well. However, some people have trouble sleeping regularly, and that's called insomnia.

Insomnia is trouble falling asleep or staying asleep. It might take a person 4 hours to fall asleep. Or they might fall asleep right away, only to wake up 3 hours later. To be **diagnosed** with insomnia, it has to happen three times a week for at least 3 months. Insomnia can make a person feel anxious and tired and put them in a bad mood the next day.

FREAKY FACTS!

Sleeping pills often don't help people with insomnia in the long run. There are often more natural ways to help insomnia. For example, exercising every day can help you sleep better at night.

THE MAN WHO NEVER SLEPT

In 1986, researchers reported on a 53-year-old man who could barely sleep. Each night, he'd only sleep about 2 hours. His two sisters had had the same problem. Two hours of sleep per night turned into only 1 hour, until the man wasn't sleeping at all. Eventually, he fell into a **stupor** and then died. Scientists realized he had fatal familial insomnia, a very rare disease that affects brain function.

WORRYING ABOUT BEING ABLE TO SLEEP OFTEN MAKES INSOMNIA EVEN WORSE.

CAN'T STAY AWAKE

While some people can't fall asleep, others can't stop sleeping! This is called hypersomnia. Most people only need 7 to 9 hours of sleep a night. However, some people can sleep up to 20 hours a day!

People with hypersomnia feel tired all the time. Even though they want to get up and go to school or work, they feel so tired, they'll fall asleep again. There have been some freaky cases in which people have slept for days.

Nathalie Hoyland, a woman from Great Britain, suffered bouts of hypersomnia beginning when she was 17. At one point, she slept nearly all day for a whole month. She only woke up to eat and use the bathroom. When she did wake, she was moody and walked around confused.

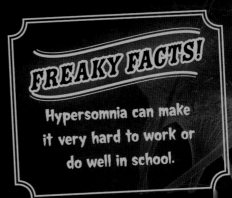

FREAKY FACTS!

Hypersomnia can make it very hard to work or do well in school.

NO ONE KNOWS FOR SURE WHAT CAUSES SLEEPING BEAUTY SYNDROME BUT IT'S THOUGHT A PROBLEM IN A PART OF THE BRAIN CALLED THE THALAMUS MAY BE TO BLAME.

THALAMUS

SLEEPING BEAUTY SYNDROME

Klein-Levin **Syndrome** is also known as "Sleeping Beauty Syndrome." It's a rare but serious **neurological** disorder. It mostly occurs in teenage boys, and one of the main symptoms is extreme hypersomnia. People who have this disorder also have an extreme drive to eat a lot of food very often, even when they don't need it. They may also have behavioral issues and trouble learning. They're moody and **lethargic**. The syndrome can last more than 10 years and is very rare. Only one in 1 million people have it!

A MIDNIGHT SNACK

Many weird things happen to people while they sleep, but some things are just plain freaky. A parasomnia is anything abnormal, or not normal, that happens to people while they sleep. One of the strangest parasomnias is sleep-related eating disorder.

Sleep-related eating disorder is very rare. People who have it go to the kitchen during the night and make themselves food—sometimes a large amount of it. They eat the food and go back to bed. It may seem like they're just up for a midnight snack, but they're completely asleep the whole time. It's very much like sleepwalking. Some people aren't aware they've even eaten, which can lead to weight gain and tiredness the next day. They might eat less during the next day and then eat a lot again that night!

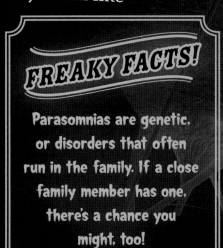

FREAKY FACTS!

Parasomnias are genetic, or disorders that often run in the family. If a close family member has one, there's a chance you might, too!

NOCTURNAL EATING SYNDROME

Nocturnal eating syndrome sounds similar to sleep-related eating disorder. It's very different, however, because people with nocturnal eating syndrome are aware of what they're doing. They may get out of bed very hungry and go to the kitchen for a big midnight snack. They're often unable go back to sleep until they eat. This can also cause weight gain and tiredness the next day. They might eat most of their food during the night instead of during the day!

SLEEPWALKING

People with sleep-related eating disorder also have another parasomnia—sleepwalking. Sleepwalking happens when a person gets out of bed and starts wandering or behaving as if they're awake—even when they're very much asleep. Have you ever sleepwalked? This behavior is more likely to be seen in children than adults, and many people report sleepwalking at some point in their life. However, **recurrent** sleepwalking is fairly rare.

Sleepwalking usually happens when a person is very tired because they haven't gotten much sleep lately. The person might be told about their sleepwalking, but they usually don't remember anything about it. They could also talk in their sleep. Sleepwalkers can become violent with people who try to wake them. Sleepwalking in your own house usually isn't dangerous, but sometimes people even wander outside.

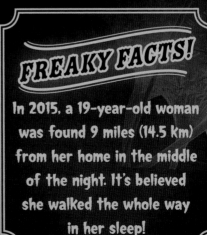

FREAKY FACTS!

In 2015, a 19-year-old woman was found 9 miles (14.5 km) from her home in the middle of the night. It's believed she walked the whole way in her sleep!

SLEEP FALLING?

In 2014, a 27-year-old man named Ryan Campbell walked off a cliff in the middle of the night. The man had been camping in a hammock and didn't know he was a sleepwalker before then. He fell 60 feet (18.3 m) off a cliff in Kentucky's Red River Gorge. Luckily, he landed on a bush, or else he would have surely died. Rescuers were surprised he walked away with few injuries.

PEOPLE WHO SLEEPWALK NEED TO BE CAREFUL WHEN THEY GO TO BED. THEY OFTEN LOCK THEIR WINDOWS AND DOORS, PUT SHARP OBJECTS AWAY, AND PUT GATES AT THE TOP OF ANY STAIRS.

SLEEP PARALYSIS

Imagine you're fast asleep in bed. You're having a very strong nightmare. Suddenly, you wake up. But you realize that you can't move at all! It's as if you're strapped to your bed. You feel something moving towards you in the shadows, and you start to panic. This **scenario** seems scary, but it's a very real phenomenon called sleep **paralysis**.

How does sleep paralysis happen? When you're dreaming, your brain is in a state called REM, which stands for "rapid eye movement." While your brain is busy dreaming, your muscles are unable to move. However, some people wake up before REM sleep is over. Even though they're awake, their body is unable to move, which can be upsetting and even cause **hallucinations**.

FREAKY FACTS!

People around the world have different ways they describe sleep paralysis. In China, they call it "Ghost Depression." In Turkey, they call it "The Dark Presser." In Mexico, they say a dead person is sitting on you.

GHOSTS, DEMONS, AND ALIENS

Throughout history, people have reported seeing supernatural beings, such as ghosts and aliens—especially at night. Many people even say aliens have taken them away from Earth during the night. Do you think these things actually happened? Many scientists think these people were actually experiencing sleep paralysis. When they wake up, but are unable to move, their brain tries to interpret the signals it's receiving. This sometimes causes hallucinations of what the person is scared of, such as demons or ghosts.

SOME PEOPLE THINK SLEEP PARALYSIS COULD EXPLAIN SOME OF THE VERY STRANGE THINGS THAT HAPPEN TO THEM AT NIGHT.

REM SLEEP BEHAVIOR DISORDER

Sleep paralysis occurs when a person's body becomes unable to move during sleep. But what if the body could move? Some people suffer from REM sleep behavior disorder. It allows them to act out dreams, which are sometimes wild and scary. They might kick and punch the air—or the people—around them. They might even jump out of bed and try to run or fight something in their dream. Many people talk, yell, or cry out during the event.

REM sleep behavior disorder is very rare. It happens when the nerve pathways that should shut off a person's body during REM sleep don't work correctly. This disorder happens most commonly with men aged 50 years or older.

FREAKY FACTS!

The movements a person acts out during REM sleep behavior disorder are called dream-enacting behaviors. They can be dangerous to a person's sleeping partner.

THE FIVE STAGES OF SLEEP

STAGE 4
NREM, DEEP SLEEP, BODY BUILDS MUSCLES AND BONE, REGROWS AND REPAIRS TISSUES

STAGE 1
EYES ARE CLOSED, EASY TO WAKE

STAGE 3
NREM (NON-REM SLEEP), DEEP SLEEP, HARDER TO WAKE, BODY MOVEMENT SLOWS EVEN MORE

STAGE 5
REM SLEEP, HEART RATE AND BREATHING SPEED UP, EYES MOVE QUICKLY BEHIND EYELIDS, MUSCLES PARALYZED, BRAIN IS ACTIVE WITH DREAMS

STAGE 2
LIGHT SLEEP, BODY TEMPERATURE DROPS, HEART RATE SLOWS, BRAIN WAVES SLOW

MORE ABOUT REM SLEEP

You might think there are only two states of mind: awake and asleep. It can feel as if sleep is like an "off" switch. However, it's not that simple. In fact, there are five stages of sleep. REM sleep is the last stage. It first happens about 90 minutes after you fall asleep, and it happens several times a night. In REM sleep, your brain creates dreams. Signals are sent to your body to keep it from moving. REM sleep activates the learning and memory parts of the brain, which helps people remember more information.

EXPLODING HEAD SYNDROME

Imagine you're asleep in your quiet house. Then, suddenly, you hear a very loud *bang*. It doesn't come from outside. The loud noise is coming from *inside* your head. That's what happens to people with exploding head syndrome!

While people as young as 10 years old have experienced exploding head syndrome, it usually happens to people middle-aged and older. It causes extreme fear for people who experience it. The loud noise can sound like a gunshot, explosion, or cymbals clashing.

Exploding head syndrome may sound really scary and dangerous. However, people who experience it don't feel pain. Doctors don't know what causes it, but stress and sleep **deprivation** may play a part.

FREAKY FACTS!

Researchers believe exploding head syndrome happens because of a kind of "hiccup" in the brain as it's shutting down to go to sleep. This hiccup creates sound hallucinations.

SOME PEOPLE THINK EXPLODING HEAD SYNDROME IS RELATED TO HEADACHE SYNDROMES. EXPLODING HEAD SYNDROME, HOWEVER, DOESN'T CAUSE PAIN LIKE HEADACHES.

HOW COMMON IS IT?

People once thought exploding head syndrome was rare and only happened to people over 50. However, a 2015 study published in the Journal of Sleep Research found that cases were much more common. Researchers studied 211 college students to judge their experience with exploding head syndrome and found that 18 percent had experienced it at one time in their life. Around 16 percent experienced it more than once. More than 36 percent of people with exploding head syndrome had also experienced sleep paralysis.

FREAKY HALLUCINATIONS

Most nights, people go to sleep and wake up normally. But sometimes, people see, hear, or feel things that aren't there. This can cause fear and confusion. There are two kinds of sleep hallucinations: hypnogogic and hypnopompic.

Hypnogogic hallucinations happen as a person is falling asleep. As their brain slips into the first sleep stages, they may see or hear something that's not really there. People often report seeing something in their room, such as a ghost or other supernatural being.

Hypnopompic hallucinations happen as a person is waking up. Both kinds of hallucinations can happen with sleep paralysis, as REM sleep makes them unable to move. Hallucinations can be very freaky, especially if a person recognizes that they're not just dreaming.

FREAKY FACTS!

Sleep hallucinations might happen because of stress, anxiety, drug use, or an inability to fall asleep. They can be very freaky!

HYPNIC JERKS

Sleep hallucinations may involve a feeling of falling and then a sudden jerk of the body. This is called a hypnic jerk, or a "hypnogogic jerk" or "sleep start." Hypnic jerks happen as the muscles are relaxing for sleep, but the brain is still firing. Some people don't even wake up. However, others may have the beginnings of a dream, or see of flash of light, and then jerk awake in a panic. While some people feel like they're tripping, others feel like they're falling to their death.

ONE THEORY FOR HYPNIC JERKS SAYS THEIR CAUSE IS **EVOLUTIONARY**. WE MAY JERK AWAKE BECAUSE WE EVOLVED FROM PRIMATES THAT SLEPT IN TREES. IF THEY RELAXED TOO MUCH, THEY FELL!

CAN YOU CONTROL YOUR DREAMS?

It may feel as if you have little control over your dreams. It's as if you're watching a movie. However, some people practice lucid dreaming, which is dreaming while they're aware of dreaming.

People who lucid dream often want to have some control over what they dream. While some can exercise control over their dreams, others may just be able to realize they're dreaming and still follow the dream's path. In a dream state, it may seem like anything is possible. You can fly or breathe underwater. You can hang out with your favorite celebrity or spend the day on a beach in Hawaii. Lucid dreaming may help those who have nightmares because they can realize they're only dreaming. It can also grow a person's creativity.

FREAKY FACTS!

One way to try lucid dreaming is to look at details all around you. Once you realize a detail doesn't line up with real life, you'll know you're dreaming and may be able to control it.

JUST AS IT'S HARDER FOR SOME
PEOPLE TO EXPERIENCE LUCID DREAMING,
IT MAY BE HARDER FOR SOME PEOPLE TO
BE HYPNOTIZED. IT HELPS TO RELAX
AND TRUST THE HYPNOTIST.

HYPNOSIS

Controlling and focusing the mind is also a goal of hypnosis.
In hypnosis, a person is awake, but usually extremely relaxed.
A hypnotist often starts by relaxing their subject. Once the
hypnotist relaxes their subject, they suggest different thoughts,
feelings, or behaviors to the patient. Some hypnotists use hypnosis
for entertainment at parties, but many are trained medical
professionals. They use hypnosis to help people overcome bad
habits, such as smoking, or mental health issues such as anxiety.

NARCOLEPSY

Often it's hard to stay awake during the day, especially if you didn't sleep enough the night before. However, people with narcolepsy experience extreme daytime sleepiness all the time! Narcolepsy is a brain disorder that makes it hard for someone to control their sleeping and waking states. They experience extreme tiredness during the day, even when they're talking or eating a meal. Narcolepsy leaves people with low energy and fatigue and keeps them from doing normal things, such as having a job.

Most people with narcolepsy have an even freakier symptom—cataplexy. Cataplexy is sudden muscle weakness. A person may be standing or walking one moment and fall to the floor the next! The person is still awake, but looks like they're sleeping. Cataplexy can last from about 30 seconds up to 2 minutes.

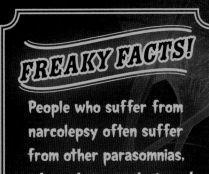

FREAKY FACTS!

People who suffer from narcolepsy often suffer from other parasomnias, such as sleep paralysis and hypnogogic hallucinations.

A CATAPLEXIC ATTACK CAN HAPPEN WHEN A PERSON FEELS SUDDENLY SCARED OR ANGRY. LAUGHTER IS THE MOST COMMON CAUSE OF THESE ATTACKS.

THE DANGERS OF NARCOLEPSY

Narcolepsy can be a very dangerous disorder. Narcoleptics have to make sure they don't put themselves into dangerous situations when they might have an attack of sudden sleepiness or cataplexy. If they suddenly drop into a cataplexic attack or fall asleep, they could harm themselves and others. Narcoleptics may have trouble driving, walking across the street, cooking, swimming, or taking care of babies. They need to know what causes their cataplexic bouts, such as laughter or loud noises.

SLEEP WITHOUT BREATH

We all have a different sleep style. Some people sleep with their mouth open or snore really loudly. Others even talk in their sleep. But did you know some people actually stop breathing in their sleep?

Sleep apnea is an **involuntary** loss of breath when someone is sleeping. A person with sleep apnea may stop breathing hundreds of times each night. In some cases, they stop breathing for over a minute! This is very dangerous and can lead to many health problems, such as heart disease or stroke. People who have sleep apnea are usually very tired during the day because their body doesn't get enough sleep at night. People with sleep apnea don't always wake up when they stop breathing, either!

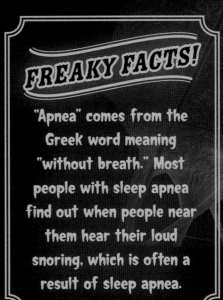

FREAKY FACTS!

"Apnea" comes from the Greek word meaning "without breath." Most people with sleep apnea find out when people near them hear their loud snoring, which is often a result of sleep apnea.

WHAT CAUSES SLEEP APNEA?

There are a few kinds of sleep apnea. Obstructive sleep apnea happens when a person's airway is blocked. A part of their throat may collapse when they sleep. In central sleep apnea, a person's brain doesn't send the signal to breathe. Some people have a mix of the two. Sleep apnea can happen to anyone, but especially to men who are overweight and middle-aged. Many have to sleep with a machine called a CPAP.

TREATING SLEEP DISORDERS

No two people sleep alike. While many can feel rested after 6 hours of sleep, others need 9 hours. You might be a quiet sleeper, but your brother or mother might snore or even talk in their sleep! For people with sleep disorders and parasomnias, their own bed can be a very freaky place. They may feel like they have little control over their sleep or the strange things that happen to them when they close their eyes.

Luckily, there's help for people with sleep problems. First, they should visit their doctor. A doctor might be able to figure out the problem, especially if it's caused by stress or another kind of medical issue. Doctors may send patients to a sleep center, where professionals can learn what happens in a person's brain as they sleep.

FREAKY FACTS!

Around 10 percent of Americans suffer from a parasomnia. They're most common in children, but many people actually outgrow them as they age.

A NIGHT AT A SLEEP CENTER

For people scared of sleeping, the thought of trying to sleep while hooked up to machines can also be a bit freaky. Luckily, most sleep centers try to make people comfortable with a soft bed and perfect temperature for falling asleep. Nurses stick patches with electronic parts called electrodes on the person's head, arms, legs, finger, and chest. The sensors record what's happening in the brain, as well as the person's heart rate, eye movements, and blood pressure. The information from the sleep study helps doctors understand the person's disorder so they can find the best treatment.

WITH THE RIGHT TREATMENT, EVEN THE MOST RESTLESS SLEEPERS CAN ACHIEVE DEEP SLEEP, WHICH IS IMPORTANT FOR STAYING HEALTHY AND BEING PRODUCTIVE DURING THE DAY!

GLOSSARY

deprivation: the state of not having something needed

diagnose: to find the cause of a problem, or to recognize a disease by examining someone

disorder: an unusual mental or physical condition

evolutionary: having to do with the process of animals and plants slowly changing into new forms over thousands or millions of years

hallucination: something that seems real but doesn't really exist

involuntary: something that isn't done consciously

lethargic: feeling a lack of energy

neurological: having to do with the brain

paralysis: the state of being unable to move

phenomenon: an event or experience

recurrent: happening or appearing again and again

scenario: a description of what could possibly happen

stupor: a physical or mental condition characterized by a loss of sense or feeling

syndrome: a group of signs that together make up a common disease

FOR MORE INFORMATION

BOOKS

Currie-McGhee, Leanne. *What Are Sleep Disorders?* San Diego, CA: ReferencePoint Press, 2016.

Scott, Elaine. *All About Sleep from A to Zzzz.* New York, NY: Viking, 2008.

WEBSITES

What Is Sleep...And Why Do We Do It?
faculty.washington.edu/chudler/sleep.html
Read about the science behind sleep, including the five sleep stages and why they're important.

Why Do I Need Sleep?
kidshealth.org/kid/talk/qa/sleep.html
Learn about the importance of getting a good night's sleep here!

INDEX